Spatial Thinking

3 Laboratorium

A series of volumes published by:
Lucerne University of Applied Sciences and Arts – School of
Engineering and Architecture
Tina Unruh, CC Material, Struktur & Energie in Architektur

Spatial Thinking

Materials' relevance to design

Dieter Geissbühler

Quart Publishers Lucerne

Spatial Thinking
Volume 3 of the series Laboratorium

Editor by: Lucerne University of Applied Sciences and Arts – School of Engineering
and Architecture, Tina Unruh, Competence Centre Material, Structure & Energy
in Architecture
Author: Dieter Geissbühler
Photos by the author: p. 24 bottom, 41, 44, 45, 47; all full-page images
(descriptions listed on page 77)
Graphic Design: Quart Publishers, Lucerne
English translation: Benjamin Liebelt, Berlin
Lithos: Printeria, Lucerne
Printing: Freiburger Graphische Betriebe, Freiburg D

First edition in German, 2012 (ISBN 978-3-03761-041-1)

Quart Publishers Ltd.
Denkmalstrasse 2, CH-6006 Lucerne
books@quart.ch, www.quart.ch

The architect can only create if he listens to the voices of millions of people and also understands them, if he suffers how they suffer, if he struggles together with them to save them. He uses iron that they have wrought, he leads them into the future because he knows what belongs to the past.
Pierre Chareau[1]

[1] Taylor, Brian Brace: Pierre Chareau – Designer and Architect. Cologne: Benedikt Taschen Verlag GmbH, 1992; original text in "La Maison de Verre", Le Point, II, Colmar, May 1937, p. 51

For Gerlinde, Emilia and Maurus, who stand above material things and provide emotional support to allow me to approach the physical side of architecture.

To create forms, we must know about the materials we use. Without materials, architectural ideas will not assume their form and cannot become concrete.

In this book, however, Dieter Geissbühler declares that it is precisely that information about materials that is being lost to the same extent at which the immaterial work has grown in influence in our culture. Immaterial data streams enable a high degree of complexity, but also harbour the danger of losing the connections between information and things themselves. In this way, an essential element of form-finding has dissolved. The values of architecture are also currently shifting due to economisation and the energy problem.

In addition to observations on this phenomenon, this book looks at approaches with which to counteract it. Looking back is only complete when it is combined with a forward glance. The relevance of materials is central. So the author picks up where the last volume of our series left off, with significant individual experience and actions playing an important role. The books complement each other and present a condensed image of our work in research and teaching. Moreover this text provides the reader with important insight in the world of Dieter Geissbühler's thought. Avoiding abstract descriptions, he addresses the nature of things directly, thus following the logic of his own arguments.

Tina Unruh, Lucerne 2012

Introduction

During these ferocious years of parenting, I usually didn't have the time, or the heart, to think about working on anything very lengthy.
… The circumstances of my life with these children dictated something else. They said if I wanted to write anything, and finish it, and if ever I wanted to take satisfaction out of finished work, I was going to have to stick to stories and poems. The short things I could sit down and, with any luck, write quickly and have done with. Very early, long before Iowa City even, I'd understood that I would have a hard time writing a novel, given my anxious inability to focus on anything for a sustained period of time.[2]

[2] Carver 1989; p. 34

What Raymond Carver states on his literary working methods and the resulting form of his literature also applies to my first substantial piece of writing. This publication was produced on the basis of my analysis in practice, teaching and research. It was above all possible through work in my capacity in the "Focus: Materials" MA course, as well as research in the Competence Centre for Materials, Structure & Energy in Architecture at the Lucerne University of Applied Sciences and Arts. Although writing is in many ways similar to the design process in architecture, it has a much greater speculative component, since its aim does not focus on a presence with a physical effect that must succeed in social use, as is the case in architecture, which can only gain its true quality in this way. There is a place in writing for the imperfectly conclusive, the fragmentary. In that sense, the following text fragments are thematically structured and follow our academic understanding, as we have presented it in Volume 2 of Laboratorium. It remains an incomplete cycle, at the centre of which lies architecture, and much more directly, the real presence of materials in architecture. It is a sketch in the best sense of the word, based on insight from experience in teaching and practical activities. The fragmentary may free the writer and the reader from the demand for comprehensiveness, but it nevertheless endeavours to sketch a comprehensive view of the significance of materials in architecture. Writing about materials means referring to the concrete, while simultaneously keeping one's eye on the complexity of possible references.

I would like to thank those responsible at the Lucerne University of Applied Sciences and Arts – School of Engineering and Architecture for granting me a sabbatical for reflection, thereby laying the foundations for this publication. My special thanks go to my colleagues in the MA course and in the CC MSE in Architecture, Christian Hönger, Hanspeter Bürgi and Johannes Käferstein, for their solidarity with my work, to my colleagues who joined me in challenging the MA students in the "Focus: Materials" course, Daniel Tschuppert, Stefan Bernoulli, Uli Herres, Roman Hutter, Yves Dusseiller and Tom Thalhofer, and above all to Tina Unruh, who not only worked with me throughout the entire MA programme, but also put a great deal of effort and intellectual energy into this publication. All of this would never have been possible without the students, who met the challenge with their own work and thereby not only kept the thought in motion, but also always opened up new paths to explore.

Finally I would like to thank everyone who made this publication possible through their financial support.

The Loss of Spatiality

The material nature of things gives them their constant and robust quality, but also causes the nature of their sensual urgency, the colourful, sonorous, hard and massive. The form is already inherent in this determination of things as materials. The constant nature of a thing, its consistency, lies in the fact that a material stands together with a form. A thing is a formed material.[3]

[3] Martin Heidegger 1977; p. 16

Although the machine, a computer and the technology behind it, gives us the opportunity to open up hyper-complex spatial compositions, we are far more strongly enslaved by the two dimensions imposed by the screen. When we try to look into depth, the screen throws it back at us. When working on our computers, we turn our backs on the physical realm and are in danger of losing interest in the sculptural effect of real things.

The interface also distances us from the real object. Space and materials distance themselves from human perception in the creative process. If they fall back on us in the real world, we feel all the more lost. We have perceived space and materials medially, have internalised a perfect image and are surprised that reality confronts us with traces of use.

On the other hand there is childish enjoyment in building, the physical resistance that we attempt to overcome with through actions. We gain insight from the haptic relationship towards objects and possible new compositions. The creative process is the intellectual precursor of a projected physical reality. It involves the development of an architectural idea through to constructed reality. The brain and the hand interact intensely and only thereby generate viable cognisance.

The tool-based flattening of the physical world goes hand in hand with other developments in the current production process of new buildings. Normative approaches with aspects of energy optimisation can lead to a creative uniformity. The ageing process, once an aesthetic merit in good architecture, is negated by the tasks of facility management, which follow a general social ideal of endless youth. The capitalisation of a building leads to the extreme economisation of building production. It is accompanied by an ever-stronger substitution principle with respect to responsibility, leading to a situation where the product guarantee replaces the system guarantee, which was once the pride of the responsible architect. The role of the architect thereby loses significant scope and it is hardly surprising that architectural work increasingly tends towards the image of an idea, neglecting the physique of the building and the entire production process.

This is all the more regrettable because the very tool that is part of the reason for this flattening also has the potential to give its physique new power. Just as Joseph Monier's invention of reinforced concrete created a new material that has inspired important developmental strides in architecture ever since, so do we face the challenge a tool poses today with respect to new spatial perception. One could draw an analogy here with the development of central perspective during the Renaissance. This new tool for digital presentation, development and production must however still reveal its potential for producing an adequate physique in the construction process, which would be an essential paradigm shift.

The virtual world is rapidly developing. At the same time – and only seemingly in a paradox way – interest in materials, the sensually perceptible appearance of our designed environment, is also growing. Materials play a central role in the development of new products and design in an architectural context. New materials and processing techniques are pioneers in the good interaction between design and engineering. The theoretic and practical analysis of the qualities and possibilities of materials forms a decisive underlying basis for the work of designers, architects and artisans.

However, changing production conditions and the swift development in materials technology make it difficult to maintain an overview. Knowledge of traditional processes is in danger of being lost. At the same time, the growing range of new possibilities is increasingly confusing.

This is where our architectural schools come into play, since it is especially their relative independence from building production that allows product-independent systems to be developed.

Conventional design methodologies will typically be based on a top-down logic; concepts and goals will be established at the outset, even before the actual design begins. The emergence of secondary elements in the design project under this regime can only be seen either as faults in the concept or mistakes that must be eliminated from the final product. [4]

[4] Reiser 2006; p.194

With top-down logic, we lose something essential that leads to a situation today where we are largely disappointed by the physique of our new buildings, even from those that can fulfil high conceptual demands.

For constructed reality, the material remains the last inherently unassailable fact, since without materials, no architecture can be created if it has physically established space as its goal.

With the loss of comprehensive material knowledge such as material properties, production, processing and its use possibilities, we increasingly lose the starting point for an architectural approach that regards the physique of buildings not as a product or object, but as something significant in our living space.

The initial situation of this turning away was industrialization, both for architecture and Modernism. It forms the point of departure, even if Bauhaus attempted in an almost romantic way to save the old tradition and transpose it into the "new times".

The materials in the construction industry have continuously, yet slowly developed further. Their use remains characterised by construction principles and building methods that only sluggishly react to changing requirements.

Nevertheless, a paradigm shift is clearly apparent with reference to the use of materials in architecture. The inclusion of grey energy and the use of closed cycles as much as possible will increasingly determine the choice of materials. Such limitations and a reversion to less technological energy requirement optimisation also give rise to the danger of a widespread loss of cultural permanence that should not be underestimated. Postmodern arbitrariness, coupled with a choice of materials that is purely aimed at effect will in future be replaced by the use of materials that fulfil sustainable requirements in a comprehensive sense. The process of enabling such assessment is however still in its infancy. To prevent that choice from simply ending in a technical argument, we need a dual approach to architecture that is designed for the polarity of "material – location": the causality of using materials and the contextual reference to built structures as an image of human action in the design process. An inversion of large and small scales in the architectural design must therefore be reintroduced. It is a way of thinking that has widely been lost since the industrial revolution, especially with Modernism, though not due to it.

Producing architecture has per se a physical origin, by actually implementing space. Beyond that, the intentions of architecture must remain metaphysical. The influence of the analysis of materials in architecture must broaden again to span the gap between fundamentals and the permeated.

Fundamentals

In 1948 I tore up a large brown piece of paper into small square scraps, which I piled up to build a rather unstable column.[5]

[5] Boetti 1995; p. 127–129

The elementary behaviour of doing, the physical production process, establishes a cultural expression. Alighiero Boetti determines this expression in an action. In his case, reverting to the elementary is an attempt to keep hold of a design expression from the everyday – in the selection of materials, the production method and the choice of objects – in a world of excessive supply and permanent medial bombardment. Expressions with a high degree of complexity are lost in the excess. Reduction is therefore postulated as a necessity for continuing life.

The direct recourse to materials in design analysis leads to fundamental insight. They lay the foundation for far-reaching manipulation without postulating absolute truth. For the design process, such insight can be the starting point and foundation for architectural analysis. They release the subsequent design steps from the context of the arbitrary, without letting the leeway for design become a limiting corset.[6] Like the status of insight from typological studies and therefore the recourse to morphological and typological rules, as especially postulated for architecture by Aldo Rossi, insight generated from analysing material properties can determine parameters that are relevant to design.[7]

[6] See the analysis of design mechanisms in the Case Studies in Laboratorium 2
[7] See the analysis of design systems by Jean Prouvé in the Case Studies in Laboratorium 2

In this sense, the questions concerning fundamental behaviour in architecture form the basis, not the reaction, to the surplus of image worlds and images. It is precisely that excess and the resulting mentality of anything-goes that has decisively contributed to the loss of knowledge of fundamental behaviour in architecture. The escape either moved towards Minimalism (which uses minimum means, mostly strongly focusing on the immediate effect of the material, in an attempt to postulate irrefutable truths) or moved towards an apparent hyper-complexity with a hardly controllable amount of information. In both cases, masterpieces have been produced that seem to give the relevant position its raison d'être. However, the fact that imitators and above all marketing for such buildings announced such truths, compromises their value. Buildings always take a stance, they take a stance in its narrow and its broader sense and are therefore speculative per se. If they do have architectural quality, they shed light on fundamentals. In this context, a recourse to the archaic is interesting, as it repeatedly reoccurs in history. *Archaisms seem to form a kind of permanent counterpoint to our culture, which takes away none of its cleansing power to open one's eyes.*[8] This was declared by the editorial team of the magazine Werk, Bauen + Wohnen, which referred to the fact that a recourse to the archaic, to the elementary, can tap a 'special power' and, as Marc-Antoine Laugier put it, can, *through orientation towards it (…) avoid fundamental mistakes and achieve true perfection.*[9]

[8] Werk, Bauen + Wohnen 3-2008; Verlag Werk AG, Zurich; Editorial, p. 3
[9] ibid.

Primitive homes, with their elementary behaviour, remain untouched by the helplessness of needing to develop coherent formal relationships within today's cultural diversity. They are as it were the distillation of a much more complex normality that we see everywhere today. These are fundamental types of behaviour that must be readdressed today, because the constructed reality no longer seems to be oriented towards it. A comprehensive reglementation of building has also contributed to this situation, leading to the assumption that simply fulfilling rules is legitimate in itself. It may sound banal to say that this practice alone is insufficient to create architecture, but it is hardly communicable in legal terms. If a building should fulfil architectural demands, it must maintain its individuality and contain generally applicable aspects within its uniqueness.

Where and how do I place a building? What connection does it have to the ground, the topography and the landscape? Which structure in its appearance accords with appropriate communication with the outside world? These fundamental questions are context-related and lead to a situation where each building must be an individual solution. Herein lies the cultural expression of and through the building and therefore the value of architecture as cultural heritage.

Hut or Cave?

A cave appears in front of him, he slips inside and congratulates himself on his discovery. But this abode also brings new unpleasantness. Around him it is dark and the air he breathes is unhealthy. He leaves the cave, determined to use his cleverness to overcome the merciless, unyielding nature. Man wishes to create an accommodation that shelters without burying him under it. (…)

This small rustic hut, (…), was the model from which all the marvels of architecture stemmed. By coming closer to the simplicity of this original model when building, one can avoid making fundamental mistakes and achieve true perfection.[10]

[10] Laugier 1989

In his manifesto on Classicism, Marc-Antoine Laugier addresses a spatial understanding in architecture from which design behaviour can be derived. However it is also clear that the hut has not remained the only source. Architectural space is a complex phenomenon that is often considered in intellectual discourse today. Aldo Van Eyck's call to replace the term "space" with "place"[11] may stem from the fact that space as a term in architecture has been subjected to comprehensive interpretations, thereby losing its understandable, clear meaning. Such over-layering with ultimately representative suggestions has contributed to formal arbitrariness in times of cultural diversity. At the time of Semper, the aim was to anchor that canon of formal representation as a generally accepted theory in society by means of supreme intellectual performance. The idea was that the hut at the origin of architecture was helpful, since it was difficult to ascribe comprehensive cultural values to a cave. The cave as a "vessel" was difficult to change from its original form and there was hardly any need for craftsmanship. Applications were mainly carried out through drawings or, with the exception of a few representative buildings, elaborate stone buildings, above all to make the space conform to the use. By contrast, the hut was made by human hands and therefore allowed representative ma-nipulation in every step of the work. The design intention going beyond technical aspects could be integrated into the production process, especially since each craft encourages one to sound out the leeway for design during the process. However the origins of

Marc-Antoine Laugier: Frontispiece. In: Laugier 1753.

[11] "Whatever space and time mean, place and occasion mean more. For space in the image of man is place and time in the image of man is occasion." Aldo van Eyck. In: Strauven 1998; p. 359

architecture lie neither in the hut nor the tent, nor even the cave. At best they oversaw the development of architecture and its fundamental principles. They are all united by the elementary desire for a space that shelters people. Their significance beyond that lies in their specific uses. An ongoing desire to design only emerges when there is a desire to express this immanent meaning. Evidence of this can be seen in the autochthonous[12] building types, as they repeatedly appeared in different forms when settling in new areas, which were developed out of the conditions of the location. They are building types that followed the availability of means in the search for protection from inhospitable natural conditions. Caves provided existing spatial vessels, could be found in rocky regions and only fulfilled to a limited degree the desired spatial dimensions and form. The argument of poor air given by Marc-Antoine Laugier cannot be unequivocally applied. For instance the cave cities in Cappadocia, where the conditions were very pleasant, became permanent dwellings.

Wood as the basic material of a tent or hut could only be found in forest areas and required craftsmanship to process it. Stone construction needed a great deal of craftsmanship, but withstood the element of fire, which was integrated into dwellings at an early stage as a provider of energy, because in addition to protection requirements, levels of comfort also determined the form of the accommodation. Autochthonous building types emerge from the optimization of local conditions, so the origins of architecture lie both in the cave and in the hut. However the core statement of Marc-Antoine Laugier, that great mistakes can be avoided by moving closer to simplicity, remains valid today. Simplicity lies in the way we handle existing materials – their extraction, processing and finishing.

The Splüi, Early Alpine Building Types
Interesting examples from among prototypical original dwellings are mixed types, as represented by the Splüi in Alpine cultures. These are buildings at the foot of large, often projecting cliffs (German: Balmen) or beneath broken off rocks that already formed a cavern, which were developed using structural additions in broken stone. This type of dwelling can above all be found in the side valleys of

[12] "long-established, indigienous, down-to-earth" according to DWDS, Berlin–Brandenburgische Akademie der Wissenschaften; last amendment 2011-06-06; in architecture, the term refers to buildings that were especially derived from mainly agricultural structures, using locally available materials that could be efficiently processed by standard craftsman's techniques.

the Tessin, in an area of agriculturally useful fields in the high Alps. Splüis were built in wild regions that could only be farmed with great effort, enabling seasonal use as accommodation, stables and storage space. The primary aim was to create a protective dwelling that could provide shelter to people and livestock in these Alpine regions where the weather changes quickly.

The fact that the buildings provided a relatively good room climate for storing food was a welcome side-effect, as well as the fact that in the height of summer, the buildings could serve as pleasant retreats with more measured temperatures.

The found, framed "emptiness" is reinterpreted through human measures and turned into space. This vessel allows a use that is oriented towards the demands of sustainability.

Splüis are therefore hybrid buildings. The search for usable, protected spatial segments represented the starting point, rather than a building as a unit that was autonomous from the context. They were only turned into closed rooms through an additional partially encompassing shell. Each of the spatially formative decisions is characterised by a specific locally-conditioned efficiency. Formal leeway is entirely subjugated to that aim. Representation does not exist.

This archaic "authenticity" was received as "romanticising" in the second half of the 20th century. In the collision between the over-instrumentalisation of the will for design expression and the further development of expressive abstraction in Modernism, architectural jargon has lost precisely that significance.

The Splüis refer to a language that still seems comprehensible in the existing confusion of architectural language. The underlying knowledge seems to be embedded in its archaic nature and can provide orientation as a safe level of retreat in layer upon layer of eras that follow.

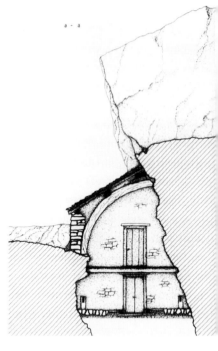

Splüi, Val Bavona. In: Buzzi 1997

Building Above the Tree Line
Buildings are immobile. They are firmly fixed to the topography, even if the structure releases itself from its natural location. Architecture is primarily created through the interaction between an ordered accumulation of material and the landscape. It is not only something artificial in itself, but also makes its context artificial.

Splüi, Val Bavona. In: Buzzi, Giovanni (Ed.): Atlante dell'edilizia rurale in Ticino. Valle Maggia. Lugano, Edizioni Scuola Tecnica Superiore 1997

[13] Loos 1982; p. 28

[14] Taut 1919; Folio 13

Grand Dixence

Almost at the same time, two important protagonists of Modernism used the mountains as points of reference for their architectural reflections. On the one hand there was Adolf Loos, who referred to "hut building artists" and therefore the fundamental simplicity of building. In an article he published in 1913 entitled "Rules for those building in the mountains", the building method of the farmer, the "substance attained through the wisdom of ancestors", should be decisive. According to his credo, traditional construction methods should only be changed if that "represents an improvement". The mountains are an image of the truth based on functional derivation: *Do not think of the roof, but instead of rain and snow. In the mountains, that is how farmers think and therefore build the flattest possible roof using the technical means at their disposal. In the mountains, the snow may not slide down when it wants, but when the farmer wants. The farmer must be able to climb the roof without risking his life in order to remove the snow. We too must create the flattest roof possible using the technical means available.* [13]

On the other hand, five years later, Bruno Taut declared:
The rocks live. They speak: We are organs of the Earth deity – but you worms – yes – so are you. You hut building artists are only in the process becoming artists! Build us! We do not wish to be merely grotesque. We wish to be beautiful through the spirit of mankind. Build world architecture! [14]
The image of architecture in the Alpine region is therefore seen by Taut as a 'global' image. Even before Modernism, it was no longer a pure image of regionalist integration. The mountains have long been a projection surface for comprehensive worldviews: idealised nature, nativeness, wilderness, overcoming natural forces and so on. One example is Bruno Taut's image cycle "Alpine Architektur" published in 1918. It refers to the mountains as a projection surface for approaching the divine.
These two positions reflect the field of tension with respect to the mountains. Building above the tree line, if the result is to have any permanence and be economically viable, must always follow elementary rules. Otherwise building in the mountains lacks a reference to a building context and therefore direct cultural integration.

The shape of the topography, with its mighty presence, becomes a breeding ground for ideas of an ideal type of building, which should be planted in a kind of paradise, inhospitable though it may be: It is a symbol of Utopian seizure of ultimately uninhabitable territories. Interestingly this field of tension has inspired very specific architectural formulations that are not independent of their zeitgeist, but have emerged with a certain degree of autonomy.

Three architectural positions in the Alpine region serve as examples of this: Franz Baumann in Austria, Carlo Mollino in Italy and Jakob Eschenmoser in Switzerland.

Franz Baumann, born in 1892, made a significant contribution to architecture in the Alpine region, especially through his Nordkettenbahn cable car stations in Innsbruck, which were built in 1928. He was familiar with the vocabulary of Modernism as a former employee in the office of Lois Welzenbacher and his buildings became an independent interpretation of the new type of construction task as a result of tourism. The formal vocabulary is derived from the technical requirements and seeks accentuation in its relationship with the Alpine context. This can already be seen in the volumetric

Adolf Loos: Landhaus Khuner.
1929–1930. In: Kristan, 2001

disposition, which is increasingly free, the higher the altitude. It is an image of a release from the constructed context and is implemented in a spatial disposition in the summit station, which is purely derived from the functions of the cable car entering it and the flow of movement of its passengers. Especially at this location, it creates a formal approach to the context of the amorphous mountain world. It remains distant from all folkloristic posturing, but also from any formal games.

Like Baumann, the buildings by Carlo Mollino are situated in a Piemont environment. Born in Turin in 1905 and better known for his diverse activities in the fields of design, erotic photography, motor racing and aviation, his quantitatively and spatially limited architecture is nevertheless remarkable. His approach can be explained by quoting an article by Bruno Reichlin:

[15] Bruno Reichlin. In: Daidalos Nr. 63, 1997; p. 28

Above all I demand the ability to dramatize a structural, constructive invention and stage its use, as provided when building 'in extreme conditions'.

Because the 'extreme conditions' provide technical difficulties, a hostile climate, altitude, an overhanging cliff, as it were on a silver plate as a

Bruno Taut, Alpine Architektur. In: Schirren 2004

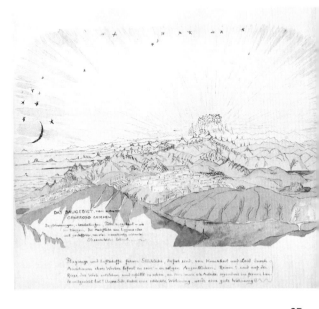

Franz Baumann, Nordkettenbahn, 1928.
Source: Bundesdenkmalamt Österreich

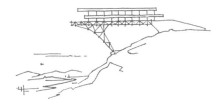

Carlo Mollino, construction sketch,

"Bauen am Berg". In: Daidalos 63 1997

mighty pretext determined by the context for an expressive design.[15] For Mollino, it is therefore explicitly the expressive excessiveness of the task and topography that should provide a "mountainous" form.

These two exponents of Alpine architecture are joined by Jakob Eschenmoser from Switzerland, a former employee in the agency of Rudolf Salvisberg. As an experienced mountaineer, long-term member of the Swiss "Alpenclub" (SAC) and specialist in cabin construction, he was able to erect a large number of accommodation buildings for the club, all with identical concepts. His projects pick up on the stone construction of the SAC's very first cabins. Availability and therefore reduced transport requirements determined the choice of materials of these original building types. Subsequently, construction physics aspects led to an increasing number of wooden buildings, which involved relatively complicated transportation, but due to their light-weight nature and prefabrication, enabled more economic implementation. Eschenmoser's reinterpretations, which used the "Planurahütte" by Hans Leuzinger as their exemplary model, are characterised by polygonal, asymmetric ground plans, optimizing the spatial use. For Eschenmoser, there are also analogies to the rocks themselves, which are highlighted by the many-angled roofs. The unusual appearance combines with the exterior quarry stone walls, the wooden interior walls and the entrance terrace to create typical characteristics. The maximised interior space, with minimal exterior finishing, may be a central requirement for building in the mountains. Eschenmoser played an important role in the history of cabin construction by the SAC and the new Monte Rosa cabin can clearly be regarded as a reference to his work. In a further development of Eschenmoser's premises, bivouacs were built in the 1960s as a reduced type of accommodation for remote, rarely visited areas. New materials were used for this purpose, such as for the "Biwak am Grassen" by Hans Zumbühl on the Titlis, with its spatial framework of steel tubes, based on a twisted hexagonal construction. The triangles were originally filled with plywood panels, but were later replaced by metal plates. Eschenmoser himself also reacted to the changing underlying conditions with his "Bertolhütte", as well as easier transportation through helicopter flights. The polygonal ground plan remains the starting point, but the building volume is newly created using a wooden frame construction that is clad in Eternit and accentuated more strongly than its predecessors through its upwardly striving roof.

The same recurring themes are applied depending on the level of technical development and with different weighting. As early as 1882, Julius Becker-Becker wrote an essay entitled "On the construction of club cabins for the SAC", calling for wooden buildings due to their shorter construction periods, the ability to prefabricate them in the valley and because of the simple transportation of manageable individual parts. The buildings can also be quickly heated, the humidity remains low and they can be quickly erected. The Cabane de Saleinaz, the first cabin built according to the instructions by Becker-Becker, was completed within six days. The new cabin built in 1996 (Architekten Stéphane de Montmollin/Brigitte Widmer), as a reinterpretation of the old cabin concept, was developed with storey-high, relatively small panels that were defined by the transport capacities of the helicopter. To increase stability, the panels were staggered like masonry stones and ordered in a composite structure. It is a simple cube, with its narrow side facing the predominant wind direction to reduce the wind-exposed surface area, without a projecting roof. The construction took 3.5 days.

Even earlier, building above the tree line was an element of comprehensive infrastructure, for instance hostel buildings as accommodation along the trade routes. The "image" may as a result have been characterised by an architectural language that only sought a reference to local building forms to a limited extent. The mechanisation of the mountains as a result of 'industrialisation' through tourism, or the construction of military facilities, also had 'global' design characteristics. They also refer to the situation that the functionally determined form is an important element of the design. This became especially relevant when power plants were introduced to the region in the 1950s and 1960s, which entailed the comprehensive expansion of infrastructures in the Alpine region. That increasingly compromised the natural image of the high Alps and the mountains were gradually encroached by an urban lifestyle. The SAC cabins are important evidence of the development of those

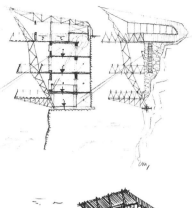

Carlo Mollino, sketches: Förggenbahn summit station. In: Daidalos 63 1997

Hans Leuzinger, Planurahütte, 1929. In: Bucher 1993

Jakob Eschenmoser, Domhütte, 1957. In: Eschenmoser 1977

New Monte Rosa cabin, joint project by the ETH, SAC, Lucerne University of Sciences and Arts, Engineering and Architecture, and the EMPA, 2010. Photo: U. P. Menti, HSLU – T&A

Hans Zumbühl, Grassenbiwak 1969. Photo: Alex Lempke

times. Alpinism itself is a result of urbanisation. It is hardly surprising that the Alps are described today as an 'urban exercise tool'. The current expansion of the SAC's range of cabins reflects that development and also raises controversial architectural questions. In a context that is 'natural' rather than built, and which is constantly reinterpreted by perspectives that are typical of the respective times, it is the tangible, constructive and functional conditions that are focused upon. The context determines the framework conditions of technical implementation. It is something that is increasingly desired in an urban context and must characterise the future of building, since calls for sustainable development should only partially be integrated into architecture. So the new construction of the Monte Rosa cabin provides viable theses on a whole series of central questions. First of all, it provides an analysis of the exact situation of the building volume, a theme that is normally predefined by the availability of the construction site, involving significant aspects of the relationship between the building volume and the territory. They are joined by themes of logistics, construction, increased requirements of ideally closed and autonomous cycles of energy and water, the influence of digital production methods, high quality transport, assembly processes and many more.

The new construction of the Monte Rosa cabin should be regarded from the perspective of a long tradition that has, especially in Switzerland, formed around the construction of SAC cabins. It contributes important aspects to architectural discussion, which reach far beyond the specific task and address fundamental issues of architecture.

The student project at the start of the development for the new Monte Rosa cabin already has this fundamental concept within it and the formal idea contained a great permanence in the development process. It marks the significance of traditions, which are available as potential in the continuous further development of historical insight. As Adolf Loos says: "Changes in the old construction method are only permitted if they represent an improvement. Otherwise, stick with the old. Because the truth, be it hundreds of years old, has more of an inner connection to us than the lie that walks beside us."

The almost laboratory-like situation of building in the high Alpine region, where much that affects architectural study occurs in a heightened form, leads to a special focus on the use of materials. Their production, transport and permanence in extreme situations are key factors in determining their choice. At the same time, the appearance of the materials characterises the relationship to the context to a degree that is rare in an urban context: the building as an individual object within the landscape. As a counterpart to the natural, the building is determined by its materials, by the strength of its contrasts.

Left top:
New Monte Rosa cabin, upper storey floor plan, new building ETH. © 2008 ETH Zürich
Bottom left:
Jakob Eschenmoser, Domhütte, upper storey floor plan, 1957. In: Eschenmoser 1977 Domhütte
Bottom right:
Stéphane de Montmollin, Brigitte Widmer, Cabane de Saleinaz. In: Daidalos 63 1997

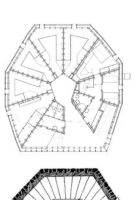

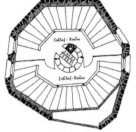

Permeation

Creating space means breaking through. In other words: not letting oneself be closed in. Not recoiling. Keeping boundaries permeable. Not letting them harden. Enhancing in an interpretive way. Not letting oneself as a user-resident-recipient be impressed, and instead referring to what exists to another space outside it in a permeable way. Man is a traject that can be activated in way that lets him play with what exists. But in it, he seeks the condition that goes beyond it.[16]

[16]Baier 2000; p. 70

Architecture is above all created by fulfilling expectations of permeability. In this respect, the physique of a building has a permeable quality, something transcendental. In it, one can find the permeation of the complex world of human existence: on a first level via opening, in the sense of omission, and on a second level through the wall as a material boundary. Hermetic construction principles required for energy reasons in today's architectural study make this second level hardly an object of architectural study at all. It is considered good construction to make the wall an impenetrable shield. Materials as the medium of mediation between a wide range of perception levels are being denigrated to become a decorative detail, the wall as 'lifeless' matter. Technical measures are being used in an attempt to fulfil the dream of a building as a living organism. The matter of the wall, although it is essential for the interaction between the building elements, can be compared to a tanned hide that has lost its universally permeable property. This exchange is not only physical, but also metaphysical, i.e. it reaches beyond the physical. It basically refers beyond the technical to the social, to historical and cultural aspects in a comprehensive sense. The perception of architecture thereby becomes multi-layered and complex. The design process, which has an expression that is a form of perception intended by the author, requires the material in order to express that complexity. Materials become the cause of a design activity which architecture regards as a mediating medium, where the author, the user and the

Roland Rainer, Haus "Unter Bäumen", 1965. In: Rainer 1990

Bottom left:
Roland Rainer, Haus "Unter Bäumen", Floor plan and view 1965. In: Rainer 1990
Bottom right:
Richard Neutra (See Key, p. 37)

uninvolved observer meet each other in an abrupt way. The search for the properties of the shell cladding of dwellings is interesting for the design process, as is the resulting significance for the user. The properties of the shell beg the question of the nature of the boundary between the interior and exterior worlds, thereby defining the perception both of the people living inside and those outside. These two terms alone mark shifts in meaning, from being laid down to lying down, down to the vertical position of the standing or walking observer. In the building, these two positions merge. The building mediates between these worlds: one inner world that tends towards intimacy and one observing world that seeks interaction.

Only the permeability of the wall links the building to its context, opening up the possibility of mediation. The wall, as a carrier of the connotations of materials, thereby stands between the town and the building. It belongs to both in the sense of a mediator. It provides protection and sympathises. For observers, it becomes the third skin and thereby creates the social embedding that is important for everyone. The design challenge lies in using the creative articulation of materials to counteract the latent tendency of buildings, and therefore individuals, towards autonomy, not just in the today's widespread form.

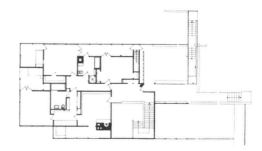

Limiting, Excluding or Connecting?

Spatial qualities are event realities. Spatial parameters such as 'inside-outside' are effects, ambulatory values within living space. In that sense they are events in a field of effects of materials, forms and significance. The quality "inside" for instance lies not in a specific material, such as grooves or boards, but instead lies in the type of connection. That quality is an event. It is therefore transient. Inside and outside are codes and can refer to everything. They are ambulatory values. They are connected to a culture and ways of life.[18]

There is no inside and outside per se. Inside and outside are forms of analysis.[19]

The spatial boundary, generally a wall, is a projection surface for events that constantly change. Only in the strictest functionalism are these events regarded as rationally describable. They are neither constant nor fully foreseeable.

The material thereby becomes the mediating element. It is permeated as a carrier of significance in itself and integrates itself to become an element of an overall spatial permeation.

Openings in the spatial boundary – windows and doors – are definitive for that permeation. Here, great constructive effort must be made, since that permeation nevertheless remains the boundary

Richard Neutra, Lovell House, 1927–1929.
In: Sack 1992

[18] Baier 2000; p. 55
[19] ibid.

Bottom left:
Richard Neutra, Lovell House, floor plans, 1927–1929. In: Sack, 1992
Bottom right:
Richard Neutra, Lovell House, 1927–1929.
In: Sack 1992

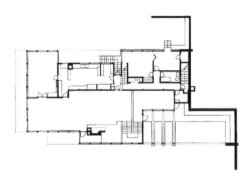

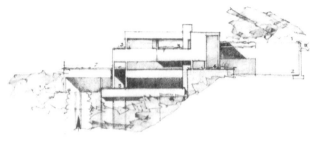

for specific functional aspects, such as the need for protection on several levels. Materials for walls, floors and ceilings articulate the type of permeation; they refer to the continuity between inside and outside, or between sequences of rooms, which can carry both the interior and exteriors conditions within them.

The Settlement as a Collective Text[20]

Buildings should be viewed as narrated stories – as if the buildings were telling stories about living and museums were telling stories about pieces of art. That approach means that the piece of work is always regarded from two perspectives: One refers to the content, the story that is narrated; the other relates to the expression, the way in which the story is told. (...)

Both the above-mentioned aspects in architecture become typological content and a compositional system: One presents the story told by the building and the other represents the discourse on it.[21]

In discussing Carlo Scarpa's architecture, when Sergio Los says that buildings tell stories, it is helpful for understanding the effect of new measures to the texture of a settlement. The settlement is a collective text that is written over a long period, sometimes continuously, but at others intermittently. This text also has another quality, because it is always read as a fragment and mostly in alternating order. Typology research in architecture attempts to unravel insight from the structure of buildings for design activities and going beyond that provides indications of morphological structures on settlements. This search for the type and order of the elementary building blocks of a settlement is directly linked to a recourse to the city.[22]

Typology determines the structure of buildings and has a direct reference to materials, especially those of the primary load-bearing structure. If one follows the theses of tectonic, comprehensively good architecture, this primary structure forms the relevant origin of tectonic form-giving. In his book "Grundlagen der Architektur. Studien zur Kultur des Tektonischen",[23] Kenneth Frampton presented this aspect in an especially pointed way. The high status of the tectonic in contemporary architectural discourse in theory and

[20] lat. *textum*: "fabric, structure"
lat. *textilis*: "woven", "worked"
lat. *textura*: "texture"
[21] Los 1995; p. 7f

[22] This especially became significant in the book by Aldo Rossi: Die Architektur der Stadt.
[23] Grundlagen der Architektur. Studien zur Kultur des Tektonischen; Munich & Stuttgart: Oktagon Verlag, 1993

criticism, though unfortunately less in constructed architecture, is no doubt a significant reflection of the desire to make the legibility of buildings the central condition of independent identity, which can prevent the increasing alienation of the user.

Today, the question of the material's relationship to the context is mainly left to the personal preferences of the individual architect or the owner, or is regulated by questionable, nostalgic legal requirements, almost always for emotional reasons (heritage preservation, uniformity etc.).

The perception of buildings is decisively determined through materials and their processing and finish. However a cultural history of materials in architecture hardly exists, or rather has been very much neglected in recent decades. A few references to architecture can be found in the work of Monika Wagner[24], who is primarily at home in the visual arts. In our cultural environment, it is above all the space outside intact old settlement cores, which have a mainly nostalgic nature with respect to their materials however, that remains unresearched. Only in the field of monumental preservation – and for protected buildings and at best their direct vicinity – is there a consciousness of the significance of materials. A research field should be structured in a way to ensure comprehensive sustainability by developing assessment criteria out of a perception-specific image and prioritising design aspects in the sense of cultural classification. Regional differences in building culture, which can be seen to this day, inherently require distinctive observation.

With the knowledge that architecture tells stories and the fact that the wall stands between the building and the city, it becomes clear that materials have a comprehensive significance. They are information carriers, like words, and use comparison, syntax, to create relationships with significance that transcend their physical appearance. Although fixed, generally valid 'grammatical' rules do not exist. The building leaves an inkling in the observer and if that can be inserted into a context, it creates meaning.

[24] Prof. Monika Wagner is an art historian and teaches and reseraches at Hamburg University, especially on the significance of materials in art, specifically in the 20th century.

Carlo Scarpa, Brion cimitero, 1970–1972. In: Dal Co 1989

The Crime Against the Ornament

While the ornament, robbed of its metaphysical-normative-political reason, could only be poor decoration, as soon as one no longer measures art by that reference system, the way is cleared for a rehabilitation of the free, autonomous ornament. The normative vacancy into which the ornament has slipped, has therefore considerably contributed to the autonomy of art, i.e. its foundation through itself, opening up entirely new perspectives.[25]

[25] Barck 2002; p. 669f.

Adolf Loos' pamphlet against the ornament was a radical statement for an architecture that should omit everything that cannot be rationally referred back to a specific "technical" function inherent in architecture. Although Loos' architectural work contains a distinctive language, it postulates the separation of form and function. Only a form derived from a utilitarian function is architecturally valid. By contrast, Frank Lloyd Wright's differentiated statements postulate a distinction between the *ornament* and *decoration*.

Each ornament, in so far as it is not developed within the nature of architecture and as an organic element of that expression, spoils the entire building, regardless how clever or beautiful it may be as a thing in itself.[26] Wright considers decoration to be an element that is placed upon architecture, which remains without reference to the built reality and should therefore be banned from architecture. More clearly than Loos, Wright demands a freedom of design that is derived from the materials: *New expressive power in architecture means that new materials determine form and structures, and demand a new attitude that ultimately qualifies both as an 'ornament'.*[27]

[26] Wright 1963; p. 48f.
[27] ibid.

The radical protagonists of Modernism went one step further and postulated pure, smooth cubes as the only right answer to the challenges of the time. There was a material justice, an honesty of expression, as form was forced to subjugate itself to function. This credo was probably internalised to such a great extent because its economic justification was so easy to deliver. The functional values could be quantified, while the metaphysical value going beyond that could be ignored. It took Postmodernism to question such dogmas, although they remain dominant in the mass construction industry to this day. Postmodernism however did not revert to what Wright called the design potential of materials, instead establishing symbolic 'patterns' of basic architectural forms.

The revival of the term tectonics, especially through contributions by Kenneth Frampton, postulated the *controlled interplay between*

[28] Hans Kollhoff, in the flyer "Die Angebote", MAS Architecture Further Education Programmes by the ETHZ at http://www.arch.ethz.ch/mas/de/angebote.pdf
[29] Holl/Merx 2009

Hild und K, Belziger Strasse Berlin, façade renovation. Source: Quart Verlag

design intention and construction implementation in the design.[28] In buildings by Hans Kollhoff, who also expressed demands to return to tectonic qualities in architecture, the ornament became more significant, while still remaining referential to historical examples. Hild und K go further with some of their projects, giving back to the ornament its significance as an element of a uniform architectural expression, thereby regaining the narrative aspect of architecture.

Gagat has also assumed that narrative quality with a study of the contemporary suitability of a historical design strategy. The project known as Rokokorelevanz, which Luc Merx is carrying out with Christian Holl and Holmer Schleyerbach together with the TU Kaiserslautern (Contingency Chair), investigates parallels between today's architectural design under the influence of the computer and that of the 18th century. *This investigation of the design potential of an object is made possible through a new understanding of technology. Technology no longer generates the form, but instead pushes the freedom of design forwards through the enormous bandbreadth of possibilities, and demands a decision that is also no longer exclusively made with the choice of the material and the processing technique.*[29] The story harbours the potential of adding to design a new significance going beyond materialisation and new production possibilities. The reference to Rococo is also an appeal for multivalence in architectural appearance. The ornament, as used in the form of the rocaille in Rococo in its spatial manifestation, was an element of a design strategy in which construction and ornamental expression were grasped as a unit, the material being the carrier of that unit.

From Brick Gothic to the Chilehaus
Between tradition and experiment
In reality, the idea of the continuing energy of every artist or technician is connected to the question of luck or death. In architecture too, that investigation is doubtless connected to the material and energy; those who do not know that cannot even grasp a building at all from a static or artistic perspective. Each material must be chosen with respect to the building locations and its transformation.[30]

[30] Rossi 1988; p. 10

In the history of architecture, traditions have repeatedly developed from individual materials that determine the appearance of buildings. For instance wood has in many regions entailed a specific, technical and design character of the local architecture. That character remained geographically limited, with exports hardly taking place. Evidence of that can be seen in Switzerland, in the many different forms of rural wooden buildings, which developed in clearly limited, rather small regions.

A somewhat different tradition can be seen in brick buildings in northern Germany and Scandinavia, stretching right up to the Baltic States. The initial situation for the appearance of a material as the most common building substance, which was usual in those times, was its local availability. In the north of Germany, there was a lack of stone, while wood was also not very abundantly available. There was however sufficient sand and clay earth. To that extent it was a standard situation. However from the 12th century onwards, the Hanse system developed in the north of Germany. Originally an association of merchants, they ensured safe trade across the sea passages of the Baltic. From the middle of the 14th century, it became a league of cities to allow clear rules for trade and established itself as a potent force in times of political instability. Although it was primarily economic interests that led to their union, the influence on political and cultural aspects became increasingly noticeable. The field of influence stretched from Novgorod in northern Russia to Bruges. In parallel with the ascendency of the German Hanse, the Gothic style emerged as an architectural form of expression, originally in the Île de France. The new style influenced the architecture of the Hanse cities, where one still however preferred to use bricks as a substitute for stone. As soon as unplastered bricks were considered respectable even for representative buildings, the independent form of brick architecture emerged. Whereas in classic Gothic architecture the mason directly works the stone block on site in the workshop, in northern Germany specially formed bricks were manufactured in the brickworks for the same purpose. The bricks were manually pressed into reusable basic forms and fired, i.e. it was an outhouse process. Individual forms were extremely

Hans Kollhoff, Tivoli, Lucerne, 2007

rare and instead a relatively small number of different modules were used to derive the design. The modules varied in terms of dimension, form and the surface. The rules for the forms were determined on the one hand by the possible variations due to the relatively small size of the bricks, but also by the wide range on offer. Naturally there was interaction between the desired form and the supply of such modules, but the design itself was limited.

In Hanseatic cities, merchants built churches and representative buildings in this way. Despite adapting the Gothic formal language, a completely new form of expression was created that reflected the self-image of the union of Hanseatic cities. The specific material was revealed, i.e. used without plaster, becoming a carrier of the message.

In this context, it is hardly surprising that the icon of brick buildings in modern times came to be built in a Hanseatic city. Fritz Höger's Chilehaus in Hamburg expresses a relationship with Brick Gothic despite the modern formal language. Brick has long become an industrially manufactured building material. But because Fritz Höger used only old bricks for his building, the surface remains differentiated

Map of the extension of the Hanse region: "German Dominance of the North and Baltic Seas". In: Putzgers Historischer Schul-Atlas; Source: http://de.wikipedia.org/wiki/Hanse

even at close inspection and resists a monotone appearance. Fritz Höger's statements heightened the significance of brick on a socially definitive level, which is today often ascribed to a national level. His colleague Fritz Schumacher, co-founder of the Deutscher Werkbund and Director of Building in Hamburg between 1909 and 1933, prefers to regard this significance on a level of perception that focuses on the atmosphere. In his capacity as Director of Building, Fritz Schumacher determined brick as the standard material for his comprehensive urban planning measures in Hamburg. He thereby evaded an ideological evaluation that regarded brick as a building material that was rooted in the "people".

If we initially ask ourselves about the value of this material in relation to other building materials, we must beware of fanaticism, because an individual joy with respect to one material can make us blind in veneration and in rejection. There is no pecking order per se among materials. Natural stone, fired stone, plaster and concrete all have, when handled properly, their artistic world and their inner justification. Accomplished masterpieces have been created using all those materials.

It would be wrong and misleading to wish to support one's preference for brick building by generally disregarding another material, as has often occurred.[31]

[31] Schumacher 1985; p. 10

Left:
View of Rostock – old engraving.
Right:
Rostock Kerkhoffhaus.

And yet Schumacher nevertheless went on to stress that the choice of materials cannot be arbitrary:

If man shrugs off the shackles of the conditions assigned to him by the natural world into which he was born, we find no ambivalence in it as soon as the behaviour to which it refers no longer has any direct connection to that nature. Our diet and clothing mostly have no direct external connection to nature, from whose essence we have distanced ourselves – not so the dwellings of people. They stand directly in the framework of that nature, forming the transition between it and our released existence.

If the design of a dwelling is tangibly opposed to the natural conditions that exist in the part of the world where it stands, we experience it as ambivalent, at least as arbitrary - or it must pursue a very specific intention.[32]

[32] Schumacher 1985; p. 11

Without describing them in detail, Schumacher used natural conditions as a reference to developing technical and design know how through continuous tradition. The aim was not to repeat the old, but to permanently change the design with the set of rules of the cultural performance of a society.

However, as he describes in detail in his test, this requires a comprehensive understanding of a building material with respect to its effects, both technical and in terms of its design.

Fritz Schumacher, Hochschule für bildende Künste, Hamburg, 1913.

The Entlebuch Quirk

Entlebuch, although situated in the centre of Switzerland and surrounded by urban areas, is a region with a very low population density. It is a UNESCO Biosphere and is classified as part of the 'Napf Silent Zone' in the book 'Die Schweiz – ein städtebauliches Portrait' ('Switzerland – an Urban Planning Portrait').[33] It shows the dilemma with which Entlebuch has been confronted for centuries. Away from the economic centres, without a major tourist attraction and in a constant struggle for sufficient yield as a basis for survival, it has developed a unique culture. In Entlebuch, due to its relatively modest economic growth, there is a whole series of interesting and predominantly authentically preserved agricultural buildings.

The repertoire includes types of Alpine cabins that are differentiated according to functions: cheese storehouses, slate-roofed houses, squire's houses, old barns, silos, summer stables and wooden bridges.[34] A unique building type developed in Entlebuch between the early 18th century and the early 19th century, in which the residential building, stable and barn are all part of a compact unit. This

[33] Diener et al. 2005
Silent zones: Former rural areas that were never able to grow under the rule of the nearby cities. The Napf Silent Zone: Emmental, Entlebuch, the Lucerne Hinterland, Oberaargau and Wynental. Emmental and Entlebuch are two exceptional Swiss natural reserves.
[34] Portmann Basel 1935

Flüeli farmhouse, Entlebuch

hybrid use conglomerate reveals comprehensive thought that throws up interesting questions in its main features, especially in today's discourse on sustainable construction.

The introduction and spread of this building type probably occurred at a time when all-year farms moved up into higher regions. This entailed building on ground that inevitably had steeper topographical conditions. Coupled with extremely limited economic means, it became necessary to conceive as compact a building volume for farmhouses as possible. The result was a very plausible distribution of uses both in terms of functions and energy, in a building volume that was optimised both with respect to its construction and the material requirements. Existing heat sources were ideally positioned in relation to the residents' use units and the abundant farming product of hay was laid over these units as a layer of insulation. Although this sounds idealising, it is a layer that changes with the heat cycle. During the coldest time of the year, in the early winter, the layer is thick. Towards the spring, it reduces as temperatures rise. The stable adjoining the residential section to the side of the ground floor is only separated from the residential area by a relatively thin wall and thereby acts as a neighbouring buffer zone. Inside the residential area, which has two or sometimes even three storeys, there are room chambers grouped around the fireplaces and stove, so that all inhabited rooms make the best possible use of those heat sources.

Flüeli farmhouse, Entlebuch. FLoor plans, section and façades. Survey by students at the HSLU – T&A

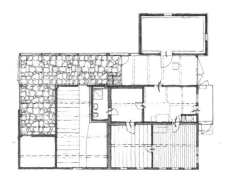
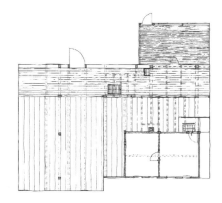

The building structure is based on the skilful craftsmanship in carpentry that is oriented towards efficiency, whereby the ideal use of the raw material was self-evident, from the chopped tree trunk to the slabs and planed wooden panelling that was used in a very targeted and limited way.

After the heyday of farmhouse research in the 1970s and a minor revival of the regionalism debate in architecture in the 1980s and 1990s, only monumental preservation seems to be interested in autochthonous buildings today. This is extremely regrettable because it is especially such buildings, however simple they may appear to be, that show an ability to bring complex connections in a structural form that can be described as sustainable. They are carriers of cultural identity, high quality craftsmanship and going beyond that, are optimised as far as possible in terms of energy. It is surprising that the Entlebuch farmhouse from the second half of the 19th century still has a design quality, one which was not appreciated everywhere at the time of its emergence. The asymmetric expression did not conform to the formal conventions of the time. It seems that form followed function earlier than one might expect and that an independent vocabulary was part of local self-understanding and the desire for autonomy.

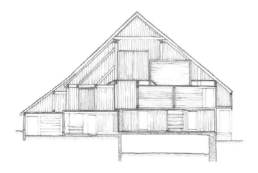
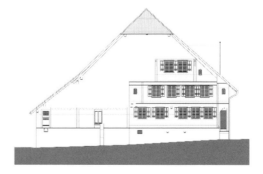

Material and Constructive Innovation

We assert the primacy of material and formal specificity over myth and interpretation. In fact, while all myth and interpretation derives from the immediacy of material phenomena, this equation is not reversible. When you try to make fact out of myth language only begets more language, with architecture assuming the role of illustration or allegory. This is true not only of the initial condition of architecture but actually plays out during the design process in a similar way. Material practice is the shift from asking "what does this mean?" to "what does this do?" [34]

[34] Reiser 2006; p. 23

If one regards constructed reality, outside formal playfulness or ideologically based self-representation, little new substance can be detected. A well-founded study of the effective creative process of buildings, the interaction of the design process and the physical implementation can hardly be perceived apart from standard solutions defined by the market. Today's study of an overall system for a building must go beyond the ordinary and release itself from the observation of individual phenomena. The interplay between the building elements, energy management, design and production must be studied in their interaction, even if that contradicts the structure of our construction industry. Hybrid systems are in many cases more effective than 'pure' ones, which hardly exist anyway and at best portray an appearance of purity. Despite a clear trend towards formal unification, hybrid systems should also be aesthetically disclosed and formally sounded out. For in future, architectural discourse will continue to be forced to take an aesthetic stance. It would be desirable if it could be integrated into the cultural context and thereby simultaneously make the physical creative process legible.

Many of today's standard construction principles in building are characterised by an additive system structure geared towards individual building products. The absurdity of autonomous layering (30 cm and more insulation layers) fixed protective layers, and countless foils etc., sub-constructions that could bear entire buildings, is becoming increasingly visible. That means that an integral effect of the constructive overall system of a wall is hardly noticed. Herein lies enormous development potential, especially because the activation of building elements could be improved by the interaction between the various layers.

In architecture, the primary focus is on space and the interaction between spaces as vessels of human action. We can only approach them through their 'boundary', which is created by materials. Construction thereby points far beyond solving technical and construction physical conditions. The effect of spaces is defined by the joining of materials.

Material: *Unlike matter and matrix, the term describes natural and artificial substances intended for further processing. Material is therefore the initial substance of every artistic activity.*[36] What Monika Wagner wrote in the Foreword to her book "Das Material der Kunst – Eine andere Geschichte der Moderne" with respect to art can also be applied to architecture. And as in the theorising on and reception of art, one must find that the handling of materials, apart from the visual effect of the surface, has only had a modest status in architecture in recent decades. The few systematic publications on materials have primarily been from the perspective of construction engineers or materials scientists. To date, there is no overview for architects that takes the significance of the choice of materials, including the cultural significance, the sensual perception such as haptics, smell, colour, surface structure and construction-physical specifics into account. Autonomous material research that only limits itself to technical or design alteration possibilities of the relevant materials makes little contribution to further architectural development. It becomes a means unto itself and comes close to a form of arbitrariness. The possibilities in developing new materials, developing traditional materials further or reusing older materials must be placed in a superordinate relationship to architectural behaviour. Construction as a set of rules of joining must once again be regarded as a central element of the design process. Otherwise architecture remains the graphic representation of an idea. Knowledge of production processes for building materials, manufacturing processes

[36] Wagner 2001; p. 12

in producing materials and assembly processes allow spatial perception that goes beyond the plasticity of a building volume and are permeated by the complexity of the requirements for architecture.

Since everything has a spatial effect, space already begins with materials. Materials create proximity and distance. They lift the space and pull it downwards, make it simultaneous or simplify it. Regular geometric surfaces and bodies are contorted by materials to create topological forms. Spaces already exist within materials. They can be unfolded.[37]

[37] Baier, 2000; p. 98

Attempt at order

Translation of the German definition in the Duden dictionary:
Ma / te / ri / al [das; -s, -ien] from Late Latin materiale, neuter noun from materialis "substantial things of matter, raw substance", cf.: 1. Substance, working matter, raw substance of which something exists, is made. 2. [written] information, documents, receipt, proof or similar. 3. Tools, objects required for specific work, to produce something, as equipment or similar.[38]

[38] Source: Duden, Das Große Fremdwörterbuch. Mannheim, Leipzig, Vienna, Zurich: Dudenverlag 2003

The physical manifestation of buildings is a central part of architectural study. Space only exists through its perceptible limitation. It is therefore the form and appearance of that boundary that determines the quality of all architecture. If one attempts to decode the building, an extremely complex system, inevitably and practically one's first thoughts are on its materials and therefore the physical conditions of the boundary. The material of the spatial boundary stands between the inside and outside; inside as a closed area, within a protective and therefore intimate shell, outside as an excluded area, as the threatening, but also public, collective living space.

Material as a primary component of the overall system stands in interaction with practically all system components of a building. This mutual influence makes the choice of materials in architecture a system-based conclusion and must release itself to a great extent from decisions of taste. Architecture thereby addresses important underlying conditions for sustainable solutions, which however can only be responsibly implemented through cultural integration. The building as an individual component stands within a larger system, namely the settlement, which is a highly complex heritage of collective authorship. It must fulfil all levels of sustainability – social, economic, ecological and also cultural.

53

The Development of Materials

The history of human development is closely connected to the availability of materials and the level of skill in processing substances into building materials. Early historical periods were therefore also named according to the mainly used material of the time. There was the early, middle and late stone age, the copper age, the bronze age and the iron age. The ability to use materials and tools determined the level of civilisation.

Initially, basic human needs such as food, health and shelter had to be provided. The field of shelter includes dwellings and therefore architecture.

According to Gerhard Auer, the development of materials can be classified into the following periods:

Natural materials: Natural building materials that are very close to raw materials, such as wood, stone and formable earth substances
Optimized materials: Optimized material properties through mechanical or chemical processing
Tailor-made materials: Materials made for a specific use
Intelligent materials: Materials that react to changes and can adapt to changing framework conditions

Applied to the building industry, there are 6 developmental stages according to Gerhard Auer:[39]

The building materials of the original hut: Natural materials that are layered and joined without any major processing
Modelled raw materials: Materials from the local environment that are used through simple mechanical processing
Physically transformed building materials: Building materials created through physical reforming, e.g. burning lime into mortar or clay into bricks
Synthetic building materials: Semi-synthetic and fully synthetic production of building materials
Symbiotic hybrids: Through the symbiosis of different building materials, properties of individual materials can be combined to give

[39] Auer, Gerhard. In: Daidalos No. 56, 1997

the hybrids better qualities than the original materials, e.g. reinforced concrete.

Intelligent building materials: Created through biogenesis and chemomechanics, representing possible building materials of the future: 'living material', self-cleaning, self-repairing etc.

In addition to those six development stages, there is the reuse of building materials:

Recycling: Used materials are returned to the cycle and processed as raw materials for new products.

Gerhard Auer, Materials family tree. In: Daidalos 56:1 1995

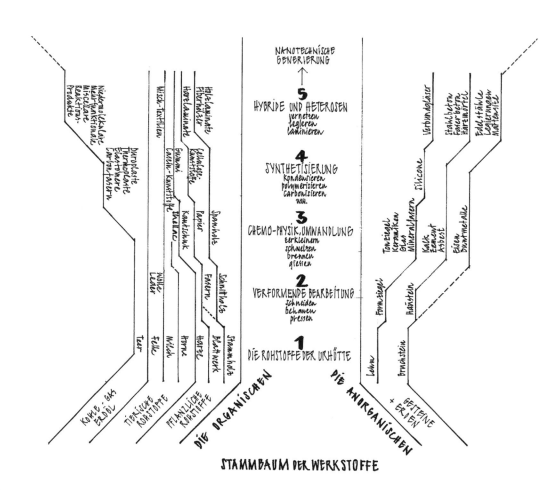

Tectonic Strategies

Construire, pour l'architecte, c'est employer les matériaux en raison de leurs qualités et de leur nature propre, avec l'idée préconçue de satisfaire à un besoin par les moyens les plus simples et les plus solides …
Viollet-le-Duc[40]

[40] Viollet-le-Duc, Eugène: Dictionnaire raisonné de l'architecture française du XIe au XVIe siècle – Tome 4, Construction

The term tectonics is used today for strongly contrasting positions and has different meanings. The underlying principle however applies that a tectonic approach is the attempt to resist arbitrary formalism – form for form's sake – and thereby attempt to develop the form out of an inner connection. This contradicts the urge towards abstraction that characterises the architectural avant garde of Modernism.

It was orthodox Modernism led by Le Corbusier that celebrated the necessity of new forms out of a postulated coherence of building technology and form. Via visual arts, it regarded the solution to be an abstract cleansing of the formal vocabulary. The fact that reinforced concrete is an extremely flexible construction method that permitted a wide range of formal possibilities, also from the perspective of the 'honest construction', can be seen in its impressive development to this day. Postmodernism also survived this urge towards abstraction and seems to have a certain resistance to stylistic transformation. Paradoxically, modern protagonists regarded form as the result not of function, but of abstraction. Somewhat more moderate positions in Modernism, such as those of Auguste Perret in France or Fritz Schumacher in Germany, who were both a little older than Le Corbusier, sought a more continuous adaptation of traditional forms and instead of producing polemical statements, left buildings that could be more easily classified as familiar and therefore have the effect of being more timeless.

The buildings of orthodox Modernism were permeated by differentiated and complex ideas that went beyond the formal and yet were by no means lost in monotony, as was the result of the global desire of the International Style of Henry-Russel Hitchcock and Philip C. Johnson, which called for a modular, repetitive architecture that created many buildings without a coherent reference to the context.

With the work by Louis I. Kahn, as well as English Brutalism, there followed a strong reaction to the 'dematerialisation' of architecture. The material was pushed into the foreground as a form of expression. For Kahn, abstraction becomes a search for the almost archaic spatial structure that seeks its image in construction. The school in Hunstanton by Alison and Peter Smithson reveals the sculptural voluminosity and coarse aesthetics of the materials used, visibly revealing how the building was constructed.

With reference to tectonic aspects of architecture, Postmodernism represented a significant break, but also an important return. The maxim of anything goes placed the form before construction, the appearance before the thing itself. The credo of honesty, which was prized almost everywhere since Modernism, was broken. The traditional formal codes become emblems and are often applied as a two-dimensional skin. On the other hand, the Regionalism debate particularly shows that the search for contextuality very often leads to a reinterpretation of regional construction methods, based on a return to history. Interestingly, during the period of Postmodernism, a movement in art enjoyed its prime that represented a radically opposing position and subsequently had a great influence on architectural events in Europe and parts of America. Minimalism, with Donald Judd as its most prominent exponent in architecture, again brings abstraction to architectural avant garde production. It is an even more radical abstraction than the International Style, albeit for the purpose of returning to the expressiveness of architectural elements: space, structure and material. Above all, the individuality of the object is now explicitly formulated.

Against this background, two 'tectonic' positions can be discerned today, with mutual boundaries that cannot be clearly defined:

In the first, architectural form is created as a result of abstraction, be it an abstraction of structure, as in projects by Valerio Olgiati and Christian Kerez, where the archaic is sought as a reference; or be it the abstraction of the uniform body by covering it with a homogenous sheath, as celebrated in some works by Herzog & de Meuron. This type of abstraction seeks to unify the building volume, thereby preventing the explicit differentiation between the construction elements in the sense of the base, wall and roof. The image of the constructive process is repressed or covered up.

The other tectonic position seeks to determine the architectural form through the production process. The expressive presentation of the constructive celebrates the technoid, albeit not in such an overt way as in times of the high-tech architecture of the 1990s. Furthermore, by reverting to traditional or historical examples, it uses an image of a familiar process to achieve something that is generally comprehensible. This can be seen very explicitly and directly in Hans Kollhoff, while other representatives of analogous architecture also reveal this aspect with a certain degree of alienation. In both cases, the form is the result of formal codes, whose integration into architectural language could not be more different.

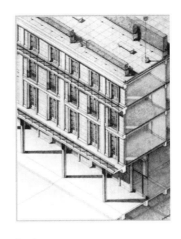

Façade structure, axonometry, reconstruction of Le Havre, Auguste Perret. In: Etienne-Steiner 2001

Hans Kollhoff's statement that physical sensibility has lost significance since Modernism and the urge towards abstraction determines the architectural form is at first glance understandable and logical from the perspective of hope for a harmonious world in the future. Representation as a demonstration of the legibility of a building and therefore the individual parts of a city has however almost disappeared in today's flood of images. Architecture still needs to be legible however and that is the great difficulty. The relevant

Alison and Peter Smithson, upper lawn pavilion, 1959–1961. In: Smithson 2001

Louis Kahn, Esherick House, Chestnut Hill, Pennsylvania, 1959–1961. In: Gast 1998

[41] http://www.arch.ethz.ch/jahr-buch08/mas_tks.pdf

[42] Geissbühler, Dieter: Revised article in Viso 02, 2009, Docu Media Schweiz, Rüschlikon, p. 38–45

[43] German definition of "Gewand" ("garment") in the Duden dictionary: origin: folded cloth
1. (eleveated) festive piece of clothing
2. (southern German, Austrian, Swiss) clothing
free.dictionary.com

[44] Petruschat, Jörg: Foreword; in: form + zweck 15; 1998; form + zweck Verlag Dorotheenstrasse 04, Berlin; p. 5

points of reference to a historical sequence can no longer be perceived. What coherent arguments are there for historical references as postulated by Hans Kollhoff? Why not use examples from a hundred years earlier or fifty years later? In fact, only the present can generate an answer that is determined by today's production processes and today's requirements. In this context, the honesty of a building could indeed be a justified demand, entering directly into the conditions of the time in which it is created, rather than an honesty of correct construction. The distinction between ordinary buildings and monuments, as is familiar to us since Aldo Rossi, is plausible. The tectonic positions must also distinguish themselves from each other in this respect. The normal should be related to the normal, refraining from exhibitionism and maintaining restraint. The abstract, for instance the technoid, has the inherent danger of a lack of contextual integration, because one is constantly confronted by a constructed reality with codes that have formed through history, even though they are continuously changing. In this sense, Hans Kollhoff is right when he writes: *If one regards tectonics as the interaction between the appearance and the constructive reality, the current relevance of the term with respect to today's architectural production becomes clear, since it presents itself as a pluralistic play on forms from corporate identity perspectives on the one hand, and as constructive exhibitionism on the other.*[41] Both positions are faced with a lack of permeation in terms of a multidimensionalism of thought and the designing and physical action derived from it.[42]

The Garment[43]

Text and texture, alphabetic and linked, numeric and synthetic, act as surfaces: The eye reads them, the hand feels the material, the paper. Text comes from a printing and layering process. Textiles come from linking operations, their appearance is not applied, but is spatially constructed. They give the hands what the text cannot give the eye: a tangible reality.[44]

In his classification of raw materials into four categories, Gottfried Semper placed textile art in first place and characterised it as "flexible, tough, highly resistant to tearing, with great absolute strength".

He regarded it to be the origin of artistic action and thereby to have a definitive effect on architecture. In recent decades, in the emerging discussion on the importance of tectonics, to which Semper repeatedly referred in many statements, textiles have achieved a significant status. However – and this may have its roots in the motivation behind Semper's hierarchy of raw materials – the formal aspect of textile design has mainly remained in the foreground. The textile was so to speak a placeholder for re-approaching the ornament and decorative elements in architecture. That allowed the condemnation of the ornament, which had already been voiced before Adolf Loos, to be revised, re-establishing the ornamental in a tectonic interpretation as relevant to design and permissible.

Donald Judd, Marfa. In: Serota 2004

If the textile behind this surface is revealed as an element of the constructive design process, it quickly becomes clear that it has hitherto and still has only received very limited attention in architecture. For instance today, one can find that the jurt as a relatively highly developed building type has hardly been developed any further. That may be related to the fact that for a long time, textiles remained very vulnerable and were therefore unable to sufficiently fulfil one of basic Vitruvian laws, namely "firmitas". From then on, textiles had the primary role of enveloping, which almost always is an aspect of decoration. Textiles thereby became an image of the ephemeral, the transient, and contradicted the demands of architecture that tended towards the long-lasting and even permanent.

So today, the use of textiles in architecture is limited to inner and outer drapes, room partitions, tent constructions, awnings and umbrellas, or as a building limited to a tent and currently to pneumatic structures.

Compared to that, textiles have undergone a technical development in a wide range of exterior construction applications, both in the production of the basic elements of the fibres and in their processing, which has fallen far behind the developments in the building industry. Although very recently, some technical textiles have achieved a high level of development in the building industry, their field of use is mostly hidden. Today's car or aeroplane seats, as well as special suits for technical and sporting applications etc. reveal construction principles that can fulfil the highest functional requirements

Valerio Olgiati, Paspels school, 1998.
Source: Quart Verlag

and are characterised by extremely precise finishing. In architecture, the interest in formal aspects of textiles has repeatedly manifested itself, for instance in Antoni Gaudi's studies on moment curves using his hanging models, textile shells by Miguel Fisac, where textile models becomes fixed form, or for example in works by Lars Spuybroek such as the Maison Folie in Lille. In addition to these formally characterised buildings, pneumatic membrane structures such as the Allianz Arena in Munich by Herzog & de Meuron are currently very popular. As a result of Fisac's interest in textile shells, interest has also been growing in recent years in the use of textiles for the casting process for concrete. Various research and development projects are currently underway to attain the formal freedom that textiles allow, making them useful both in terms of design and technology. At the University of Manitoba, Canada's Centre for Architectural Studies and Technology, such possibilities have been explored with great intensity for years. However mostly, the use of textiles in all these works remains limited to individual qualities. The potential of textile constructions is hardly used in a comprehensive way. Today, textiles could be used in construction in a much more consistent way with respect to their qualities. The design and sensual qualities of textiles could decisively enrich architecture.

Semper used textiles with respect to their inherent constructive logic as a reference for handling standard building materials. Today, our use of textiles, or rather their high level of development in production, finishing and design in fields that are not related to construction, could serve as inspiration to take a further step in the use of textile constructs. With respect to new developments in architecture, textiles have the chance to ideally apply highly complex requirements in an interactive system. As a three-dimensional matrix, they can contribute to making the targeted distribution of individual materials possible in the depth of spatial boundaries. Abstracted in the sense of bionic models, today's autonomous construction layers, which have virtually become the rule, could be developed in a homogenously effective hybrid construction[45] in which a wide range of different individual elements enter into a symbiotic relationship with each other. Requirements such as insulation, mass and also design could thereby be treated in an overall

Gottfried Semper, drawing of Treichler bathing ship, 1862–1864. In: Nerdinger 2003

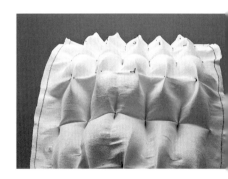

Experiments with textiles, MA course, Lucerne University of Applied Arts and Sciences, Engineering and Architecture, Photo M. Käch

[45] Homogeneously effective hybrid constructions are buildings consisting of a combination of different materials, whereby each material interacts with other functional requirements to be as useful as possible, going beyond its primary function.

Antoni Gaudi, hanging model, Colonia Güell church, 1898–1908, reconstruction of the model in 1982, Institute for Light Supporting Structures at the University of Stuttgart and by the Gaudi Group of the TU Delft

[46] Dieter Geissbühler, revised article in Modulor 3 2011, Boll Verlag, Urdorf; p. 50–54
[47] Huber 1971; p. 11

CAST, Manitoba. Fabric Formwork. The Centre for Architectural Structures and Technology, Unviersity of Manitoba. http://www.umanitoba.ca/cast_building/research/

solution approach with individual elements mutually requiring each other. For instance the dimensions of an overall system could be reduced and its material use optimized. The use of further developed production and processing technologies for textiles would also allow much more complex construction systems in the building industry, with which the requirements of adequately sustainable implementation in today's times could be fulfilled with a high level of architectural quality.[46]

The Necessity of Constructions

Development (is) only possible through findings; it is the only way it can advance. I have always avoided, even forbidden studies outside the studio: What is brought in from the outside is mostly inappropriate and only wastes time. The man at the workbench must be the first to give his opinion on a construction problem, while the draftsman must grasp with equal speed and correct his mistakes if necessary; the construction requires a continuous dialogue and collaboration. (...)
That is why I reject anticipation, which is uncontrollable later and paralyses the researcher. One should only construct what one can implement.[47]

Teaching and researching at an architecture college provides the chance to establish a laboratory situation; a laboratory in which the independence of traditional and apparently irrefutable conditions, the original underlying conditions, can be studied in the best sense of the word. This text presents approaches to such a process as fragments of a search for a new whole.

The standard construction principles 'on the market' can hardly fulfil the comprehensive requirements of 'sustainability'. The underlying energy conditions have led to a situation where construction principles are being pushed to the limit in implementation, especially in terms of economics. Minimising energy loss, as well as optimizing storage capacities, require new solutions rather than simply increasing the thickness of one's jumper, since sooner or later it will be too thick and uncomfortable. Solutions must be studied in their entire architectural significance and assessed with respect to the potential of the design and architecture. In this sense, studying the relationship between construction and design becomes the central question with reference to the sustained relevance of architecture. This paradigm shift will dominate architectural activities in the coming decades. The end of the postmodern arbitrariness of material use in architecture offers the chance to strengthen architecture as a building process, placing 'doing' clearly in front of 'design' again. And if architects regard that as the core of their activities, the status of architects as generalists will be increasingly perceived.

The desire for homogeneous wall construction, the desire for a material that can do everything, may be legitimate, but has its limits. The result of such quasi-homogeneous walls is enormous construction volumes that create a disproportion to the effectively developed space. Aesthetic coherence is a condition of quality architecture, but does not cause the seemingly manic urge for a material that can be used for everything. Striving for a homogenous appearance remains a temporary fashion. This unification, paired with a geometric purity, makes buildings so abstract that despite their perfection, they are no longer able to communicate with our senses. Abstraction always entails the danger of turning one's back on adequate production. Good architecture is based on good construction and requires coherent constructive solutions more than spatial and formal extravagance. Today's construction is predominantly a two-dimensional process; layers of components are joined together mostly without any mutual interaction. They are regarded as autonomous elements, as separate functions still dominate the field of construction. Today's construction principles are also determined by the well established, but hardly agile building industry. In that context, innovation that is aligned towards the physique of the building is definitive for the sustainable future of construction.

Handling Nature

Biological construction methods follow the principle of the most highly integrative building method: Unlike technology, biology hardly constructs with individual parts that are separately finished and then subsequently combined. Very often, almost regularly, the formal elements are created in mutual adaptation and fitting and ultimately merge to form an integrative unit.[48]

Miguel Fisac: Edificio de Usos Sociales, Madrid 1985. In: Soler 1996; p. 223

The "Glued House Project" in the 2007 MA course at the Lucerne University of Applied Arts and Sciences, Engineering and Architecture, textile construction

[48] Nachtigall, Werner: Wanzen und Brücken, Biologische Konstruktionsmorphologie und technisches Denken, in: archithese 2.02 March/April 2002

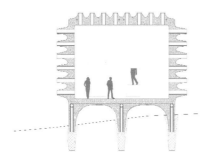

Roman Hutter, section of "the glued house", MA course 2007 HSLU – T&A

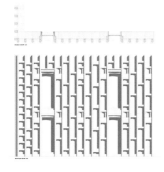

Dominique Neierlin, section and view, brick building, MA course 2010 HSLU – T&A

[49] See e.g. works by the department of Gramazio and Kohler at the ETH Zürich at http://www.dfab.arch.ethz.ch/

Is it possible to unravel 'genetic' underlying principles in architecture? What would the determining basic elements, which 'growth mechanism' would determine the joining process? How do individual parts as well as the joints influence the perception of building elements and buildings?

In this context, an analytical look at biological phenomena and speculative abstraction through drawings and models can provide a wealth of material. They allow us to release ourselves from formal or direct interpretation. Construction in biology is always an optimised use of materials in which different parts interact in mutual dependence. Ideal mass distribution, ideal alignment, maximum elasticity etc. react to a wide range of requirements. The appearance is defined by the function, but allows an enormous diversity of expression. Apparently identical requirements are given distinctive characteristics. Herein lies the importance of studying biological models with respect to architectural work. It provides points of reference on handling possible materials in a design process that is oriented towards constructive principles in architecture. The biological example provides structural insight. Architecture created on the basis of such thought achieves artefacts that do not become imitations of biological references. Building remains caught within the conditions of cultural and technical development, but can move away from traditional, standard solutions. That is so significant because on the level of computer-controlled production techniques and methods, it opens up a broad range that makes much seem possible that until recently was technically and economically unfeasible.

Until now however, little can be seen of such concrete application in the building industry. Applying some production techniques that are available from other fields would add creative freedom and provide new architectural means of expression.[49]

New production methods allow a differentiated, layered structure. Materials could be allocated to new application fields and new building materials could be developed. This requires an experimental approach, first as a speculative experiment in a laboratory studio and then in the workshop to develop prototypes. In collaboration with the (building) industry, market-mature systems could be developed further. Such laboratory situations can almost only be achieved in architectural colleges due to their research commission. As history has shown, the reality of building production is that it is extremely slow to adapt to new production principles, as the immense economic pressure robs planning offices of the means of experimenting in this field. Calls for the industrialisation of the building process are at least a hundred years old. But still we are moving in the realm of production processes by small businesses and craftsmen.

Working situation, MA course 2010
HSLU – T&A

The studio of traditional architectural practise is an image of the usual way of developing and communicating architectural knowledge. The workbench and today the even smaller surface of the screen are primarily intended for "headwork" that is manifested in draftsmanship. Model building remains an important element, but limits the dimension of the study to detailed work. The rough work of effective, physical action, the haptic and visual qualities of the materials of which the built reality exists, is almost entirely excluded from the working environment of the architect. In the laboratory however, the working situation is flexible. Work can be done both mentally and practically. Space can be changed and becomes a valuable tool for an open approach. This space thereby comes closer to the meaning of laborare (lat.), to work, to suffer, to make an effort, i.e. as a place of passion through physical and mental action. This space enables what Juhani Pallasmaa describes in his book 'The Thinking Hand' as follows: *Design practice that is not grounded in the complexity and subtlety of experience withers into dead professionalism devoid of poetic content and incapable of touching the human soul, whereas a theoretical survey that is not fertilised by a personal encounter with the pietics of building is doomed to remain alienated and speculative – and can, at best, only elaborate rational relationships between the apparent elements of architecture. But there are no 'elements' in artistic phenomena, as the parts derive their entire meaning from the whole.*[50]

[50] Pallasmaa 2009; p.146

When Pallasmaa refers to the fact that buildings represent an effort of collaboration, that increasingly applies to the design process today. Only in the joint, physical experience does a whole emerge

with meaningful parts. The immense complexity of architectural work, from the idea to the building, requires collective knowledge and collaborative action.

The laboratory situation encourages dialogue between individuals participating in a development process. Architecture is teamwork, is inter/trans/multidisciplinary and pools knowledge from a wide range of disciplines. Good architecture manages to generate quality space and a 'good' form from that knowledge. The situation in the laboratory can implement these intentions using examples. It allows the scientifically related research and speculative implementation, in which failure does not become a threat to one's survival. Unburdened knowledge and a wealth of experience released from traditional perspectives can be processed, on the basis of which it is possible to reflect on design steps. Design is thereby grasped as the generation of collective knowledge, and made plausible through research and documented reflection. Architectural knowledge only becomes communicable and continuous through the process of one's own research on architectural work. This spatial knowledge,[51] which attempts to interpret every space as a specific space, in which history can first occur in the sense of Karl Schlögel,[52] is derived from projects and the implementation of architectural intentions. Herein lies the knowledge on the properties and effect of the spatial boundary, which has priority significance. The use of materials and therefore construction is an essential condition in this creative process and forms one of the most important levels that turn the design process into a research activity.

In felting, it is essential to feel the quality of the material with one's hands. Even when one is laying out the wool, there are invisible "weak spots" where the wool is not equally dense, where holes may appear. The producer acts intuitively and uses her experience. The hand touches, feels, steers, controls and corrects the felting process. By determining the felting factors herself, the producer can have a direct influence on the final result. The felting effect can be light, i.e. loose and transparent, or firm and permeable. The difficult nature of woollen fibres is another factor, since they react differently depending on their length and elasticity, which is an aspect of the felting process that cannot be planned.[53]

Physical action in architecture is an important precondition for

Drawings, "Constructions outside architecture", MA course 2010, HSLU – T&A

[51] See Laboratorium 2, researching Architecture

[52] Karl Schlögel is a German historian who became well known through his book "Moskau lesen". He argues in favour of direct viewing as an important method of congnisance.

[53] Hauser, Angela: Filz; in: form + zweck 15; 1998; form + zweck Verlag Dorotheenstrasse 04, Berlin; p. 30

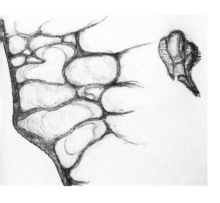

Drawings, "Constructions outside architecture", MA course 2010, HSLU – T&A

gaining comprehensive insight. The hands are an extension of the brain. They feel the resistance between the thought and the task at hand. This friction provides underlying experiences for the creative architectural process. Drawings and models are not simply objects with which to represent the concept, but also changeable organisms of speculation and reflection. They can be used to emotionally and rationally approach the physical reality of the planned building. Experience gained from hands however is usually transmitted through tools, which characterise our relationship to the material needing to be processed. Contrary to the opinion that today's increasing mechanisation of tools and their electronic controls have increased the distance between materials, the hand and the brain, the spectrum of the experience has merely shifted. In this way, the ever further developed tools represent a chance to strengthen the aspect of craftsmanship again, to give the physique of the constructed entity the necessary weight.

The future will need to strive to develop more distinguishing construction processes. Therein lies the potential for a resource-efficient approach to building. At the same time, it also harbours the hope that architects will once again manage to reclaim a decisive share in the characterisation of the physique of architecture. Architecture would thereby gain in expression. It would be revived in the three-dimensional permeation of the idea and physique.

Although materials are extremely burdened in their perception, they remain innocent per se. That represents hope that architecture will accept their unlimited potential in the future.

Bibliography

Auer, Gerhard: Baustoffe sind von Natur aus künstlich. In: Daidalos, 56. Gütersloh, Bertelsmann Fachzeitschriften, 1995

Baier, Franz Xaver: Der Raum – Prolegomena zu einer Architektur des gelebten Raumes. Cologne, Verlag Walther König, 2000 (2nd edition)

Barck, Karlheinz (Ed.): Ästhetische Grundbegriffe: historisches Wörterbuch in sieben Bänden. Stuttgart, J.B. Metzlersche Verlagsbuchhandlung and Carl Ernst Poeschel Verlag GmbH, 2002

Boetti, Alighiero: Aus dem Tagebuch (1967), in: Arte povera, Manifeste, Statements, Kritiken, Nike Bätzner (Ed.). Dresden – Basel Verlag der Kunst, 1995

Bucher, Annemarie and Kübler, Christof: Hans Leuzinger (1887–1971) – pragmatisch modern. Zurich, gta Verlag, ETH, 1993

Buzzi, Giovanni (Ed.): Atlante dell'edilizia rurale in Ticino. Valle Maggia. Lugano, Edizioni Scuola Tecnica Superiore, 1997

Carver, Raymond: Fires – Essays, Poems, Stories. Random House Inc., New York 1989

Dal Co, Francesco and Mazzario, Giuseppe (Eds.): Carlo Scarpa, opera completa. Milano, Electa, 1984

Diener, Roger/ Herzog, Jacques/de Meuron, Pierre/Meili, Marcel/ Schmid Christian, Eds.: ETH Studio Basel, Institut Stadt der Gegenwart: Die Schweiz. Ein städtebauliches Porträt; Einführung, Grenzen und Gemeinden, Materialien. Basel, Birkhäuser, 2005

Ellwood, Craig: 15 Houses, in: 2G LibrosBooks. Editorial Gustavo Gili, Barcelona, 2004

Eschenmoser, Jakob: Vom Bergsteigen und Hüttenbauen. Zurich, Orell-Füssli, 1977

Etienne-Steiner, Claire: Le Havre, Auguste Perret et la Reconstruction. Connaissance du Patrimoine de Haute-Normandie, 2009

Frampton, Kenneth: Grundlagen der Architektur. Studien zur Kultur des Tektonischen. Munich & Stuttgart: Oktagon Verlag, 1993

Gast, Klaus-Peter: Louis I. Kahn, Die Ordnung der Ideen. Birkhäuser Verlag, Basel & Berlin, Boston, 1998

Hauser, Angela: Filz; in: form + zweck 15. form + zweck Verlag Dorotheenstrasse 04, Berlin, 1998

Heidegger, Martin: Holzwege (Complete Works, Vol. 5) – Das Ding und das Werk. Frankfurt a. M., Vittorio Klostermann, 1977

Hild und K: Recent work; in: 2G, n. 42; 2007; Editorial Gustavo Gili, Barcelona

Holl, Christian/Merx, Luc: Das Konkrete und die Architektur. Vol. 14, No. 1, October 2009; at: www.tu-cottbus.de/theoriederarchitektur/Wolke/wolke_neu/inhalt/de/heft/ausgaben/109/Holl_Merx/holl_merx.php

Huber, Benedikt and Steinegger Jean-Claude (Eds.): Jean Prouvé – Architektur aus der Fabrik. Zurich, Verlag der Architektur Artemis, 1971

Irace, Fulvio (Ed.): Carlo Mollino 1905–1973. Milan, Electa, 1989

Kristan, Markus (Ed.): Adolf Loos, Villen. Vienna, Album Verlag, 2001

Laugier, Marc-Antoine: Essai sur l'Architecture. Paris, 1753; German edition: Das Manifest des Klassizismus, Zurich & Munich, 1989

Loos, Adolf: Gesammelte Schriften. 2010, Lesethek

Loos, Adolf: Ins Leere gesprochen. Vienna, Georg Prachner, 1981

Loos, Adolf: Trotzdem. Vienna, Georg Prachner, 1982

Los, Sergio: Carlo Scarpa – Hatje Architekturführer; Stuttgart, Gerd Hatje, 1995

Nachtigall, Werner: Wanzen und Brücken, Biologische Konstruktionsmorphologie und technisches Denken, in: archithese 2.02 March/April 2002

Nerdinger, Winfried and Oechslin, Werner Eds.: Gottfried Semper, 1803–1879, Architektur und Wissenschaft. Zurich, gta Verlag, 2003

Pallasmaa, Juhani: The Thinking Hand, Existential and Embodied Wisdom in Architecture. Chichester (UK), John Wiley & Sons Ltd., 2009

Pallasmaa, Juhani: The Embodied Image. Chichester (UK), John Wiley & Sons Ltd., 2011

Pérez-Méndez, Alfonso: Craig Ellwood – In the Spirit of the time. Barcelona, Editorial Gustavo Gili, 2002

Petruschat, Jörg: Foreword; in: form + zweck 15; 1998; form + zweck Verlag Dorotheenstrasse 04, Berlin

Portmann, Dr. Hans: Brauchliches und Bauliches aus dem Entlebuch; Separatdruck aus Schweiz. Archiv für Volkskunde, Vol. XXXIV (1935) No. 2/3; Basel 1935.

Rainer, Roland: Arbeiten aus 65 Jahren, Salzburg, Residenz Verlag, 1990

Reichlin, Bruno: Carlo Mollino – Bauen in den Bergen, in: Daidalos 63, 1997. Munich, Callwey.

Reiser, Jesse: Atlas of Novel Tectonics/Reiser + Umemoto. Princeton Architectural Press, 2006.

Rossi, Aldo: Wissenschaftliche Selbstbiographie. Bern, Verlag Gachnang & Springer, 1988;

Sack, Manfred: Richard Neutra. Zurich, Verlag für Architektur, 1992

Saner, Hans; Die Anarchie der Stille. Basel, Lenos Verlag, 1990

Schirren, Matthias: Bruno Taut: Alpine Architektur – eine Utopie. Munich, Prestel Verlag, 2004

Schumacher, Fritz: Das Wesen des Neuzeitlichen Backsteinbaues. Munich, Callwey, 1985

Schumacher, Fritz: Das bauliche Gestalten. Basel, Birkhäuser, 1991

Serota, Nicholas (Ed.), Judd, Donald. London, Tate Publishing, Tate Modern, 2004

Smithson, Alison and Peter: The Charged Void: Architecture; New York, The Monacelli Press, Inc. 2001

Soler, Francisco: Miguel Fisac, Architect. Madrid, Ediciones Pronaos, 1996

Strauven, Francis: Aldo van Eyck – The Shape of Relativity. Amsterdam: Architectura & Natura, 1998

Sulzer, Peter: Jean Prouvé, Oeuvre complète/Complete Works, Volume 2: 1934–1944. Basel, Birkhäuser Publishers for Architecture, 1995

Taut, Bruno: Alpine Architektur. Hagen: Folkwang-Verlag, 1919

Taylor, Brian Brace: Pierre Chareau: Designer and Architect. Cologne: Benedikt Taschen Verlag GmbH, 1992; original text in "La Maison de Verre", Le Point, II, Colmar, May 1937, p. 51

Turtenwald, Claudia (Ed.): fritz höger (1877–1949). Hamburg, Dölling und Gallitz, 2003

Viollet-le-Duc, Eugène: Dictionnaire raisonné de l'architecture française du XIe au XVIe siècle – Tome 4, Construction. 1856. http://fr.wikisource.org/wiki/Dictionnaire_raisonné_de_l'archi-tecture_française_du_XIe_au_XVIe_siècle

Wagner, Monika: Das Material der Kunst. Munich, C.H. Beck, 2001

Wirz, Heinz (Ed.): Hild und K. Lucerne: Quart Verlag, 2011

Wright, Frank Lloyd: Schriften und Bauten. Munich & Vienna, Albert Langen Georg Müller, 1963

Dieter Geissbühler

1955   Born in Basel; grown up in Kriens

1982   Graduated in Architecture at the ETH Zürich and at the Cranbrook Academy of Arts, Bloomfield Hills, Michigan USA

1982–1987   Senior Assistant to Professor Flora Ruchat-Roncati, ETH Zürich

since 1987   Self-employed in Lucerne

since 2000   Lecturer at the Lucerne University of Applied Science and Arts – Technology & Architecture

             Currently responsible for the Focus: Materials in the MA Architecture course, research focus on CC Material Structure and Energy, "New applications for textiles in architecture"

Financial and conceptual support

Special thanks to the institutions and sponsoring companies that provided financial support, which was an essential factor in the publication of this series. Such cultural engagement enhances the fruitful, friendly collaboration between construction culture and the building industry. Thank you for your cooperation.

Bless Hess AG, Luzern; Deon Architekten AG, Luzern; Elmiger Tschuppert Architekten, Luzern; Bauunternehmung Estermann AG, Sursee; GKS Architekten + Planer AG, Luzern; Walter Graf, Luzern; Keller Ziegeleien AG, Pfungen; Kost + Partner AG, Sursee; Lengacher Emmenegger Partner AG, Luzern; Lüscher Bucher Theiler Architekten, Luzern; Markus, Geissbühler & Theiler AG, Luzern; MVM AG, Luzern; Nolax AG, Sempach-Station; Pensimo Management AG, Zürich; Planteam S AG, Sempach-Station; Holzbau Renggli AG, Sursee; Rüssli Architekten AG, Luzern; Schärli Architektur AG, Luzern; Bauingenieure Schubiger AG, Luzern; Todt, Gmür + Partner AG, Zürich

Lucerne University of
Applied Sciences and Arts

HOCHSCHULE
LUZERN

Engineering & Architecture

Architecture Department

Büro für Bauökonomie

Büro für Bauökonomie, Luzern

IGD GRÜTER

ARCHITEKTUR · TOTALUNTERNEHMUNG

IGD Grüter AG, Dagmersellen

Laboratorium

Laboratorium: A study environment in which to reflect, but above all to work and experiment. It is not just for testing, but also for presenting ideas and theories, in brief – a place of research. Because *laborare* not only means "to work", but also "to make an effort" and is therefore an activity with an open end and related to research.

Edited by: Lucerne University of Applied Sciences and Arts – School of Engineering and Architecture, Competence Centre Material, Structure & Energy in Architecture, Tina Unruh

Volume 1: Climate as a Design Factor

Contributions: Roman Brunner, Christian Hönger, Urs-Peter Menti, Christoph Wieser

This volume studies the climate as a design factor and examines its influence on energy and design consequences. Instead of an abstract, technical perspective, the approach is illustrative and spatial, thereby consciously stimulating the search for inspirational solutions.

112 pages, 17 x 22 cm, German (partly in English)
ISBN 978-3-03761-010-7

Volume 2: Researching Architecture

Contributions: Andri Gerber, Tina Unruh, Dieter Geissbühler

The second volume of the Laboratorium series takes a stance in the widespread discussion on research and the creative process of architecture. Examples are used to show how individual insight can be applied to the design process, thereby making it communicable.

104 pages, 17 x 22 cm
German ISBN 978-3-03761-019-0
English ISBN 978-3-03761-023-7

Quart Verlag GmbH, Heinz Wirz
CH-6006 Luzern
books@quart.ch, www.quart.ch

Competence Centre Material, Structure & Energy in Architecture, Lucerne University of Applied Sciences and Arts – School of Engineering and Architecture
http://www.hslu.ch/technik-architektur